Hello kids
This is a message to
our beautiful children out there.
You are very very prescious
and my true inspiration for this book.
You ALL are important for a better planet,
where we act consciously
and with compassion
towards all surrounding souls:
from our fellow humans
to all creatures & animals alike.
We all serve a purpose.
And always remember:
Your happiness is true richness.
Shall this book bring
an abundance of happy moments
into your life.

Aa
...as
in
ape

COOL ape facts

The ape family is composed of gibbons, orangutans, bonobos, chimpanzees and gorillas.

Apes have the same blood type as humans, including A, B, AB, and O.

Ape arms are longer than their legs.

The great apes cannot speak.
They have a higher voice box, which is not flexible.

Great apes love TV films and videos.

Apes are omnivorous.
However, they mostly eat plants and fruits.

Apes are known to be good parents.

Apes make shelter-like-structures
using nests out of leaves, and they stay as a family.

A group of apes is called a troop.

Bb
...as
in
bee

BUZZING bee facts

During one collection trip,
a honeybee will visit up to 100 flowers.

Honeybees beat their wings 200 times per second,
creating their trademark "buzz".

There are three types of bees in every hive:
a queen, worker bees, and drones (drones are all male).

Bees fly 90,000 km to produce 500 grams of honey.

Honeybees are not born knowing how to make honey.
Instead, they are taught in the hive by older bees.

Honey is super healthy.
It contains all the necessary nutrients to sustain life.

A single hive can produce 45 kilograms of honey per year.

A group of bees is called a bike of bees.

Cc
...as
in
chameleon

COLORFUL chameleon facts

They have amazing eyes that can swivel around simultaneously in two completely different directions.

Chameleons have special color pigment cells called chromatophores, so they can change their body color.

Chameleons are reptiles with about 160 different species. They eat large insects like stick insects, crickets and grasshoppers.

They live in desert areas and also in warm habitats of rainforests.

Chameleons have feet that work like salad tongs.

...as
in
dolphin
Dd

PLAYFUL dolphin facts

Dolphins come from the whale family.

There are nearly 40 species of dolphins worldwide.

Dolphins eat up to 22 kilograms of fish per day

They are highly intelligent and playful.

Dolphins are very social with human beings.

They nurse their young ones until they are 2 years old.

Dolphins are mammals.
They come to the surface to breathe.

Humans are their major threat,
due to water pollution and fish hunting.

The group of dolphins is called a school.

Ee
...as
in
elephant

SKY-HIGH
elephant facts

Female elephants lead the elephant families.

Elephants don't need much sleep.

Elephants are considered emotional creatures.

They have an extremely impressive memory.

They are creative when it comes to communication.

Elephants have a long pregnancy of about 22 months.

Elephants can swim and love to shower.

They can also get sunburn.

Elephants cannot jump or gallop.

A group of elephants is called a herd or a memory.

Ff
...as
in
frog

JUMPY
frog facts

The frog´s skin can absorb water.

Frogs can lay up to 4000 eggs during the frogspawn.

A frog can jump 20 times its own height.

Frogs come in a wide range of colors.

The largest frog comes from Cameroon
and is known as the goliath frog.

The smallest frogs are under 1cm.

Male frogs croak to attract the females.

Frogs have teeth in their upper jaws
to hold onto their prey before they swallow.

A group of frogs is called an army of frogs.

Gg
...as
in
giraffe

SLENDER
giraffe facts

Giraffes are the tallest creatures in the whole world.

Giraffes run at a speed of up to 60 kilometer per hour.

Their necks are too long to reach the ground.
So giraffes eat leaves only from trees.

Giraffes drink water occasionally, about once every few days.

They also spend a huge part of their lives standing.

A new-born giraffe can stand up within 1 hour of its birth.

Giraffes don´t have the same spots.
Each giraffe has different spots, like our fingerprints.

Giraffes are herbivores, meaning they eat plants.

Giraffes are always in groups and are social animals.
A group of giraffes is called a herd or a tower.

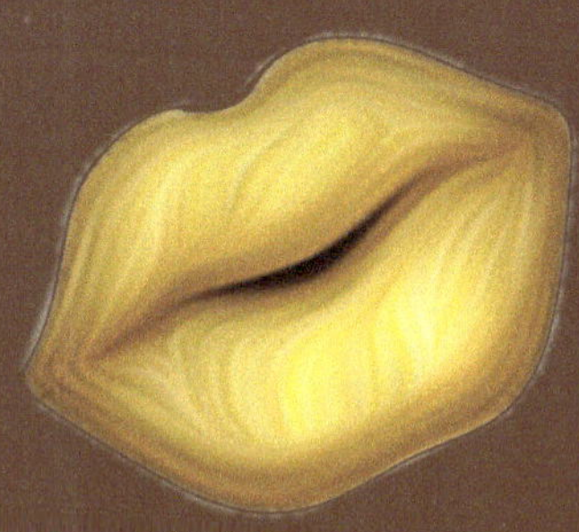

...as in hippo
Hh

Hippos can neither swim nor float in water.
They are semi-aquatic animals.

They can hold their breath for about 7 minutes underwater.

Hippos can live up to 40 years.

Hippos stay out of water for about four to five hours.

Hippos are highly aggressive.
They use their canine teeth for fighting.

Hippos are mostly active during night hours.

Hippos live in groups of about 10 to 20 hippos.

The group of hippos is called a herd, a bloat or
a thunder of hippopotami.

Ii
...as
in
iguana

GENIUS iguana facts

Iguanas are reptiles.

Iguanas are large, long-bodied lizards with long lifespans.

The heaviest iguana is called the blue iguana.
It weighs about 14 kilograms.

As herbivores, iguanas eat plants.

Iguanas are sometimes territorially aggressive.
They are curious and independent creatures.

Iguanas are known to be excellent swimmers.
They can stay underwater for about 45 minutes.

Iguanas can be kept at home.

A group of iguanas is called a mess.

Jj
...as in
jaguar

ROARING
jaguar facts

The jaguar is a big cat.
It falls under the Panthera genus.

Jaguars are carnivores. They eat meat only.

Jaguars are considered the third-largest in the cat family.

Jaguars are only located in the Americas.

They enjoy swimming, just like tigers.

They hunt, walk and live alone in densely populated forests.

Jaguars have a very powerful jaw.

The male jaguar is about 15% larger than the female.

Jaguars live up to 20 years.

Jaguars also roar.

A group of jaguars is called a prowl.

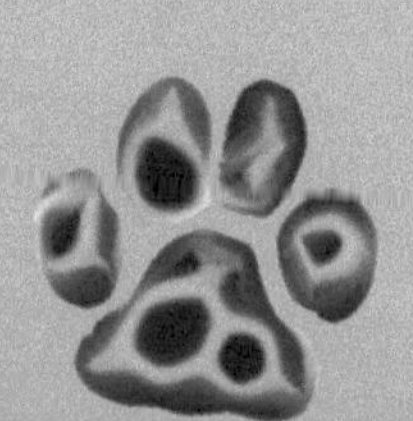

Kk
...as
in
koala

Koalas are not bears; they are simply koalas.

Baby koalas are extremely beautiful.

Newborn koalas are about 2 cm long,
and weigh less than 1 gram.

Koalas have a pouch-like feature to carry young ones.

Koalas are mostly found in eastern and southern Australia.

Their size ranges from 60 to 85 cm.

Kolas eat up to half a kilogram of eucalyptus leaves per day.

Koalas can sleep up to 18 hours a day.

They are losing their habitat due to deforestation.

Koalas stay alone and are not social animals.

...as
in
lion
LI

ROYAL lion facts

Lions fall into the cat family.
They are considered the largest of the cats.

Lions eat meat, hence, they are carnivores.

A lion´s roar can reach up to 8 kilometers away.

A hunting lion can run up to 80 kilometers per hour.

Lions hunt mostly at night
and into the early morning hours.

Lions have powerful jaws and killer teeth.

African lions are known to be social.
They live in a group called a pride.

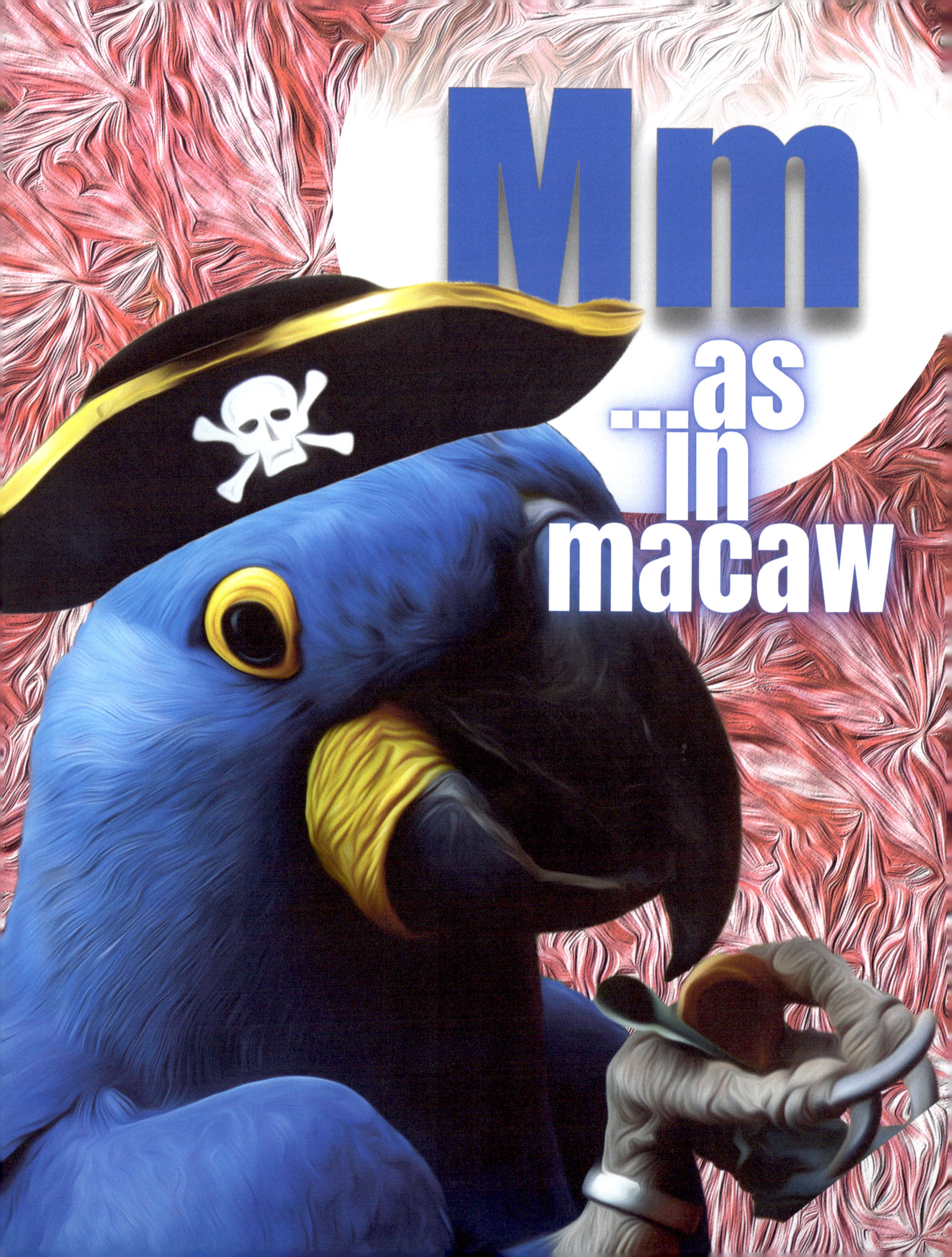
Mm
...as
in
macaw

BRILLIANT *macaw facts*

The blue macaw is the largest bird in the parrot family.
It is 1 meter in length from the beak to its tail.

The blue macaw is the most charismatic bird species.

They can get 60 to 80 years old.

They have strong beaks and are pretty loud birds.

The blue macaw eats
nuts, insects, fruits, and green vegetation.

They share their food with their mates.

Macaws are able to mimic human vocals.

They are social animals
and are mostly seen in flocks of at least 30 birds.

Macaws love to bathe.

They are among the most endangered bird species.

A group of macaws is called a flock.

Nn
...as
in
numbat

STRIPY
numbat facts

Numbats are termite eaters.

They eat up to 20,000 termites each day.

Numbats have a good sense of smell.

Their body is covered with reddish-brown fur with white stripes on their backs.

Numbats don't destroy termite mounds.

Their major predators include cats, snakes, dingos, and foxes.

Numbats live 4 to 8 years.

They are known to be solitary animals.

Oo
...as
in
otter

Otters are mainly water-based animals.
There are sea otters and river otters.

Otters are expert swimmers.

They can hold their breath underwater for up to 8 minutes.

Otters eat fish, crustaceans, and small reptiles.

They are related to badgers and weasels.

Otters have short legs and long, flexible bodies.

The fur of the otter is water-repellent,
and they have the thickest fur of any animal.

Otters are smart animals and use tools.

A group of otters is called a raft or a family.

Pp
...as
in
penguin

HAPPY
penguin facts

Penguins are flightless birds.

They have flippers which they use to swim in the water.

Penguins live in the southern hemisphere.

Penguins eat fish.

They spend most of their time in the water.

The King penguin is the second-largest penguin species.

Penguins do not have visible ears,
but their sense of hearing is very good.

A group of penguins on land is called a waddle.

A group of penguins in water is called a raft.

Qq
...as
in
quail

SMALL
quail facts

Quails are small ground birds.

The quail family have loads of different colors,
including brown, red, blue, yellow and black, amongst others.

Quails eat seeds, grain, and insects.

Quails can lay 10 to 20 eggs at one time.

They have many enemies:
Cats, skunks, foxes, snakes, owls and dogs hunt quails.
As well as humans, birds of prey, and a host of other animals.

Quails can only fly a short distance.

Quails usually live alone.
However, in the fall time they form flocks.

A group of quails is called a bevy.

Rr
...as
in
rhino

There are five different species of rhinos:
Sumatran, Javan, Indian,
black, and white rhinos.

Rhinos have horns which are boneless.

They communicate using huffs and snorts.

They are extremely fast.

White rhinos located in Africa
are the largest rhinos in the world.

They weigh up to 2300 kg.

Rhinos have a thick skin.
But their skin is very sensitive.

Rhinos have poor eyesight,
but their other senses are strong.

Rhinos live in groups called the crash.

Ss
...as
in
seal

CLEVER
seal facts

Seals are warm-blooded mammals that live in or near the sea.

Seals are semi-aquatic marine animals.

There are about 33 seal species.

Seals can live up to 30 years.

The smallest seal species is called the Galapagos seal.

Seals can sleep underwater.

They can dive up to 900 meter deep.

Seals have a familiar call
that mothers and their babies use to communicate.

Seals are carnivores and feed on fish, sea birds and shellfish.

A group of seals is called a pod or a herd of seals.

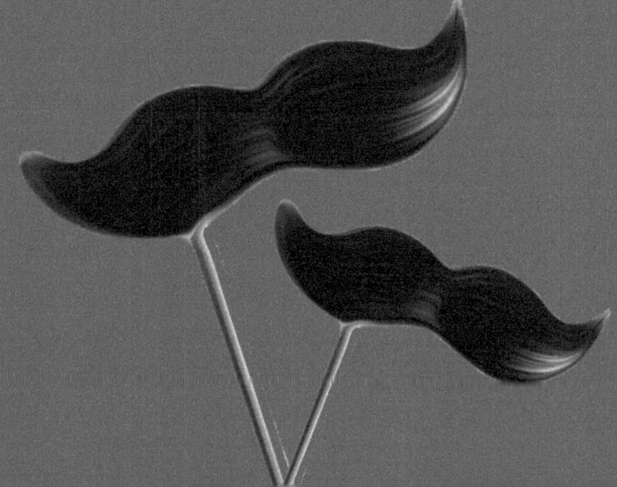

...as
in
tiger
Tt

Tigers belong to the cat family.

They hunt at night while looking for food.

Tigers eat meat only.

Tigers are extremely good swimmers.

They can run at a speed of up to 80 kilometers per hour.

One punch from a tiger can kill somebody.

Tigers live up to a maximum age of 25 years.

Tigers don't roar.

A group of tigers is known as a streak.

...as
in
urial
Uu

ROCKING *urial facts*

Urials fall in the wild sheep species.

Urial have long reddish-brown fur and weigh about 90 kg.

They are mostly found in western Asia.

Urials eat mostly grass.

Urials eat specific plants that heal them
when they are ill.

Urials have a great memory.

A group of urials is called a flock, a mob or a herd.

W
...as
in
viper

SNAKY
viper facts

Vipers are a family of venomous snakes.
The venom causes a very painful wound.

All vipers have a pair of long hollow fangs
which are used to inject venom.

Vipers are camouflage experts.

Vipers have slit-shaped pupils that can open wide
to cover most of the eye or close almost completely
which helps them to see in a wide range of light levels.

Most vipers sleep in the day and wake up at night
to ambush their prey.

Vipers are predators, which means they eat other animals.
Their main food is birds, bird eggs, amphibians, such as frogs
and toads, and other small reptiles like lizards.

Most vipers live in the tropics.

A group of vipers is known as a nest or a den.

Ww
...as
in
whale

GIANT whale facts

The blue whale is the largest in the whale family.

The weight of a blue whale is equivalent to 24 elephants.

They live for about 200 years.

There are killer whales or orcas which travel in family groups.

The smallest whale in the Antarctic is the Antarctic minke whale.

The blue whale does not have teeth.

Whales cannot eat human beings.

A group of whales is known as a pod.

Xx
...as in xantus

FEATHURED
xantus facts

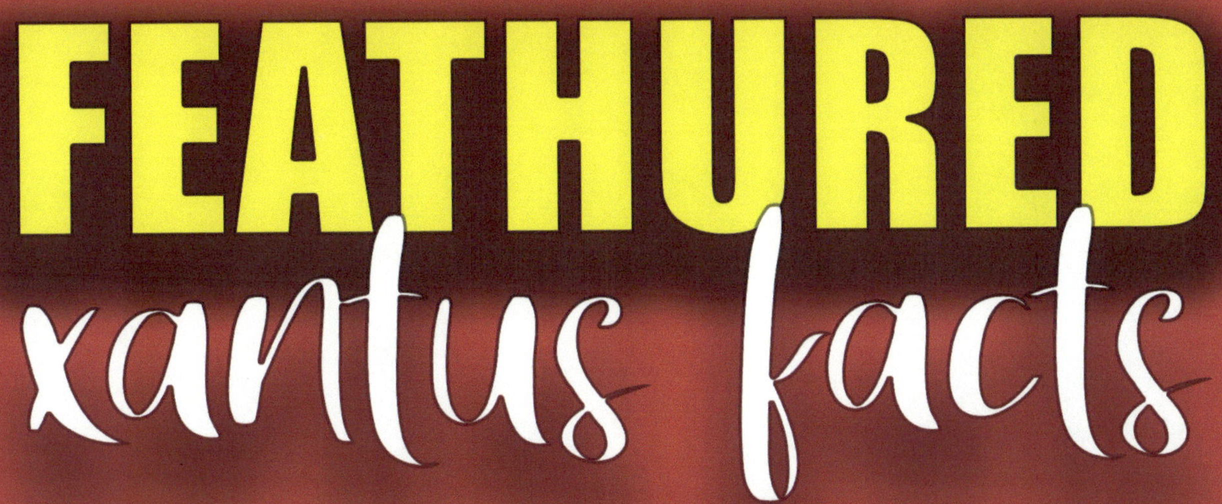

Xantus hummingbirds are extremely beautiful birds.

They grow up to a maximum length of 9 cm.

Xantus hummingbirds have long tongues and curved beaks.

They mostly feed on nectar from flowers.

Xantus hummingbirds cannot walk.

They use spider silk and lichens to make nets.

Xantus hummingbirds lay the smallest eggs.
Mostly they lay two eggs, almost the size of a bean.

They have a dark reddish-brown tail and white eye stripes.

A group of hummingbirds his known as a bouquet,
a glittering, a hover, a shimmer,
or as a tune of hummingbirds.

Yy
...as
in
yak

MASSIVE *yak facts*

Yaks are less aggressive, hence, naturally friendly animals.

They eat grass, plants, and tubers.

Yaks live in the highest altitude compared to other mammals.

The yak has more than one stomach.

They can survive in the coldest areas.

Yaks use their dense horns to break through the snow.

During summer, they shed down their undercoat.

Yaks´ milk is also used to make yogurts.

A group of yaks is known as a herd.

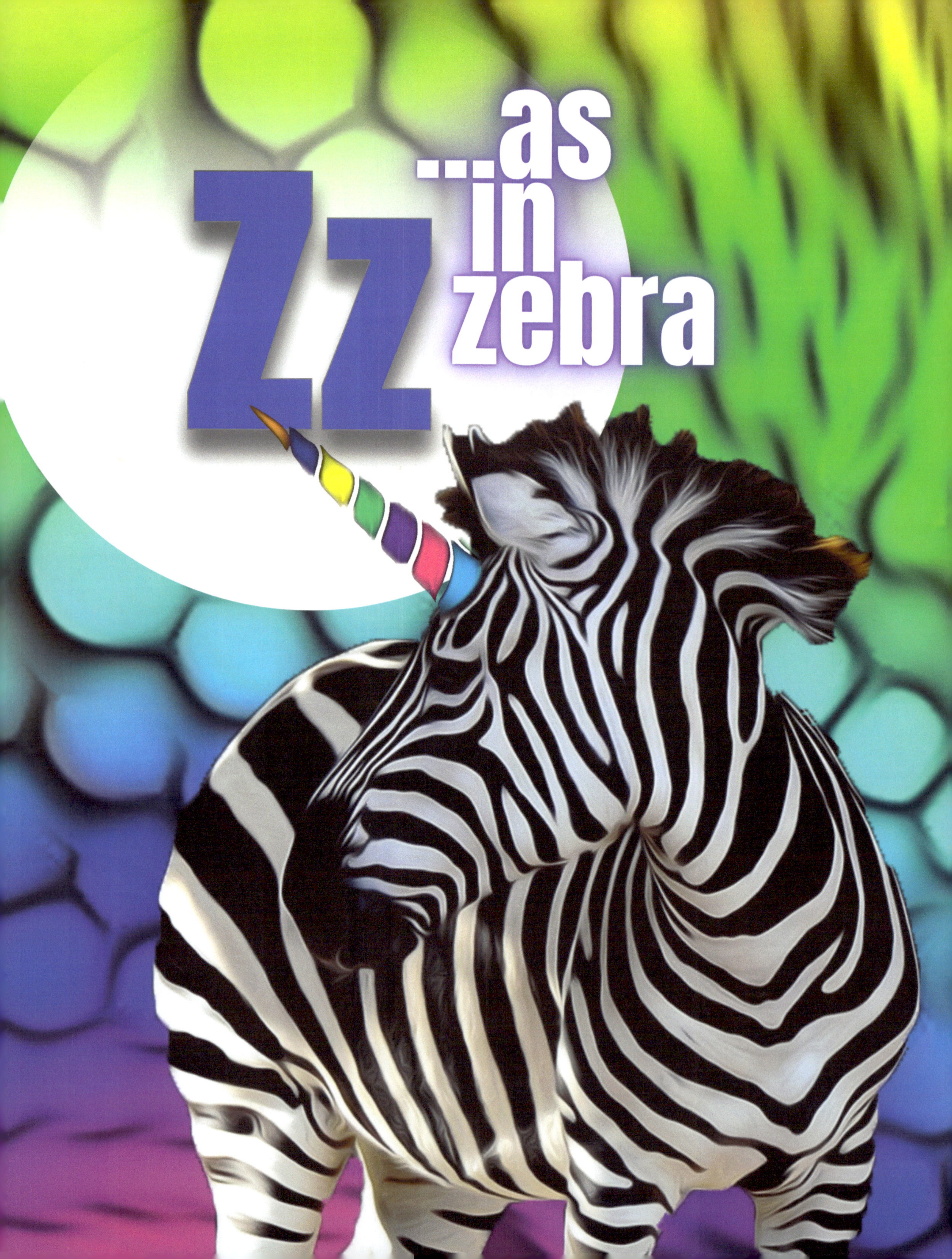
Zz
...as
in
zebra

FAIRYTALE *zebra facts*

Zebras have white and black stripes.

They fall under the same family as horses and donkeys.

Many wild zebras live in Africa.

Zebras run side by side when they are chased by predators.

Zebras have excellent hearing and eyesight.

Zebras mostly stand up when sleeping.

They eat grass.

A group of zebras is called a dazzle, a zeal or a stripe.